AVICENNA

ON THE SCIENCE OF THE SOUL: A SYNOPSIS (*FIL ILM AL-NAFS*)

ADAPTED BY
LALEH BAKHTIAR

GREAT BOOKS OF THE ISLAMIC WORLD

Avicenna On the Science of the Soul

Printed in the United States of America.

Cover design by Hafeez Shaikh

Library of Congress Cataloging-in-Publication Data

Ibn Sina, Abu Ali al-Husayn ibn Abd Allah
Psychology
    1. Psychology. 2. Medicine. I. Title

ISBN 10 (Book): 1-56744-199-8
ISBN 13 (Book): 978-1-56744-199-4

Published by
Great Books of the Islamic World

Distributed by
KAZI Publications, Inc.
3023 W. Belmont Avenue
Chicago IL 60618
Tel: 773-267-7001; FAX: 773-267-7002
email: info@kazi.org

PREFACE

This work by Avicenna was first translated into English in 1906 by Edward Abbott van Dyck. Supported by the Arabic original, it has been adapted with modern terminology.

Avicenna wrote this short treatise on the soul for a Prince as a gift to him.

ON THE SCIENCE OF THE SOUL: A SYNOPSIS (*FIL ILM AL-NAFS*)

In the Name of God, the Merciful, the Compassionate. May God bless our Lord Muhammad and his family, and give them peace. O may God facilitate [this undertaking] and have it end in good, O Thou Generous Being!

Abu Ali Ibn Sina, the chief expert, the learned and learned leader, the precise and accurate researcher, Truth's plea against humanity, the physician of physicians, the philosopher of Islam, may the Most High God have mercy upon him, says (in honor of the Prince):

The best way to begin is to praise the Giver of Strength, to invoke blessing and peace upon our Lord Muhammad, His prophet and servant, and upon the prophet's good and pure offspring. He then further says:

If it were not possible for the lowly and small to aim for great heights, it would not be possible for their to gain the help of their best qualities; to obtain a position in their service; to join their social circle; to pride themselves on having connected with them; and to openly state their reliance upon them. The bond that unites the common person with the elite would be broken; reliance upon the Book and its shepherd would end; the weak would have no chance of becoming powerful through their strength; the ignorant would not be able to gain knowledge through meeting with the wise; nor would the wise ever draw close to the ignorant.

I offer this humble synopsis on the Science of the Soul (psychology) to the Prince, may God give him long life. I pray that it be acceptable to him. I have come to the conclusion that the major virtues are two: love of wisdom through theoretical principles and intending the most honest of deeds. In this I have found the Prince, may God give him a long life, to be of worthy character. That is why I perceive that of all the presents I could

5

give him, a book on the virtues, and particularly, on wisdom would be that which he would most appreciate.

I have noted that philosophers and pious saints have held fast to the Tradition: Whoever knows himself, knows his Lord. They also say: Whoever fails to know himself is more likely to fail to know his Creator. How can anyone be trusted as a reliable authority when they fail to know themselves? Even further than this, God Almighty points out in the Quran: *And be not like those who forgot God and He caused them to forget themselves.* (59:19) Is not God's making the forgetting of self to depend upon forgetting God done so as to awaken one's attention to the remembrance of Him with the remembrance of one's self? Is not the knowledge of God bound to the knowledge of one's self, one's soul?

Even ancient philosophers followed this saying at an oracle that said: Know thyself, O human being, so shall you know your Lord. It is said that this saying is engraved upon the temple of Aesculapius whose most well-known miracle was that he was able to heal the sick through loud supplication. This is what all priests who lived in his temple did. It was from him that philosophers obtained the science of medicine.

Thus I give the Prince a book on the soul in the form of a synopsis. I ask God to prolong his life, to keep the evil eye away from him, to restore his wisdom whenever it fades, to give him strength to be able to continue.

I will only achieve my goal through God: He is the best of Helpers.

I have arranged this synopsis in ten chapters as follows:

CONTENTS

1: TO ESTABLISH THE EXISTENCE OF THE POWERS OF THE SOUL IN A DETAILED ANALYSIS AND EXPLANATION

It is first necessary to establish the existence of the powers (faculties) of the soul before defining each of them. The most important characteristic of the powers are two: motivation and perception.

In regard to motivation, it is necessary to show that every moving body has a moving cause or motive. It will then be clear that bodies in motion have moving causes that we call powers. This is in addition to natural or involuntary motion such as that which is heavy, sinking, and that which is light, rising.

In regard to perception, it is necessary to show signs or traces that perception cannot be ascribed to a body unless it be ascribed to the powers that are capable of perception.

There are things that share something in common and also differ with one another. That which they share in common is different from that by which they differ. In regard to having something in common, they share the fact that they are bodies. In regard to differing in something, they all move in different ways. If this were not so, there would not be a body at rest or the motion of a body except along a circle.

Moving in a straight line is established by the form of something showing that it will not move forward without stopping or resting. Therefore, bodies are not to be clothed with the quality of motion not because they are bodies, but because of causes beyond their physicality. An example is the footprint of someone who is walking.

We find among the bodies that have been generated from the four elements [earth, air, fire and water] that they move in two ways, there being more or less difference in how they move. One type of movement of the body is inherent in its elements causing it to move downwards by the nature of its heavy element. This kind of motion of bodies moves in one direction with a tendency to be constant.

9

The second kind of motion goes against the nature of its element. Its nature is either to rest in its natural position once it reaches that as, for example, a bird's flying in the sky in spite of its weight or a person walking upon the earth's surface.

There are two causes for these two motions. Each cause is quite different from the other. One is called natural motion and the other is called soul or power. Therefore, it is a sound conclusion to affirm the existence of the powers.

When it comes to perception, bodies share this in common because they are bodies and with the distinction that they are repeatedly perceptive. With discrimination it is clear that perception does not differ in bodies due to their substance, but rather due to their powers within these bodies. Therefore, it is clear that powers have an existence and this is what we wanted to demonstrate.

2. Division and Classification of the Powers of the Soul, and Definition of the Soul

The Powers of the Soul

It has been clearly shown above that there are some things that have one thing in common and differ in something else and that what things share in common is different from what they differ in. We found that ensouled bodies are bodies that possess a soul. They hold this in common yet they differ in the properties of motivation and perception.

In regard to motion or motivation, they both agree and differ. They have in common that they move and grow. They differ in that one set moves and grows according to the will while the other does not move such as plants.

Living beings also have in common that they both have sensation and perception up to the point of sensuous perception. After that they differ in that one set perceives sensations while another one perceives not only sensations, but has intellectual perception.

We also found that the power of motivation is more widely embracing than the power of perception and that plants completely lack intellectual perception. We then know for certain that the power which the animal has in common with the plant is more general than the power of perception and motivation which the animal possesses. Each one of them, in turn, is more general than the rational soul that belongs to the human being.

The powers can be classified under three ranks:

The first of which is known as the plant or vegetable power because of the participation therein of the animal and plant.

The second is known as the animal power.

The third, as the rational power.

Therefore, when considering the primary parts of the soul. from the standpoint of its powers, it has three types of powers.

DEFINITION OF THE SOUL

Now to the definition of the Universal Soul. It will become clear according to the tenets that I hold that among clear truths one is that all natural bodies are compounded of matter and perfection. As for matter, one of its properties is that through it a natural body is acted upon in its very self. A sword, for instance, does not cut through iron except with its sharpness that is its form. It becomes jagged due to iron, but not due to its shape.

Another property is that bodies do not differ through their matter. Earth does not differ from water through its matter, but rather through its perfection. Another example, matter does not furnish natural bodies with their characteristics that are particular to them except potentially. The humanity of a human being being human is potentially derived from the four elements, but not actually.

In regard to perfection, its particularity is that through their perfection bodies put forward their actions. As for the perfection, its peculiarity is that through it, bodies perform various deeds and actions. First of all, a sword does not cut through its iron except through its sharpness. Secondly, bodies differ one from the other only through their genus or kind. That is, the perfection, since earth does not differ from water except through its perfection, not in its matter. Thirdly, natural bodies acquire their being, what they in fact are, that is, from their perfection. In regard to the humanity of a human being, this is through his perfection and not his matter which consists of the four elements.

We say that a living body is a natural compound that is discriminated from the non-living by virtue of its soul, not by virtue of its body. It is alive through its soul and not through its body. Its soul is within it.

It is clear that what is within a thing, as long as it continues, is its perfection. Thus, the soul is a realized or actualized perfection because through it, the characteristics of things become perfect. The soul, then, is a perfection or realized identity. Actualizations or vital powers that direct an organism toward self-fulfillment are divided into two: firstly, either through the principles underlying the actions and their effects or secondly, the very actions and effects themselves.

The first is the origin and the second is the action or effect. It is in this sense that the soul is the first perfection or actualization because it is a source and not the outcome of a source. Among perfections, there are such as belong to bodies and such as belong to immaterial substances. In this sense, the soul is the primary perfection that attaches itself to a body and uses the body as its instrument.

Among bodies there are those that are artificial and those that are natural. The soul is not a perfection of an artificial body. Therefore, it is a primary perfection attached to a natural body. Again, among natural bodies there are such as perform various actions and activities through organs as well as those that do not perform their actions or activities through organs as, for example, simple bodies and those that act through the constraint of simple powers.

In other words, we could say that among natural bodies there are those whose design, among other things, is that they produce of themselves. That is, they perform the actions of animals voluntarily, of their own will, while there are those whose design, among other things, is not to so produce.

Therefore, again, the soul is not a perfection that attaches itself to the last two divisions as stated above. The complete definition of the soul is to say that it is a primary actualization or perfection that attaches itself to an organic, natural body. If we wish to say further, it is a primary actualization attaching to a natural body that has the potential of life. It is a source of the many potential actions of an animal. It is the origin of the actions done by such beings as may be living. This then is the Universal Soul and its definition which we have undertaken to show.

3. THAT NONE OF THE POWERS OF THE SOUL ORIGINATES FROM THE COMBINATION OF THE FOUR ELEMENTS BUT COMES UPON THEM FROM WITHOUT

Among all the things that are compound or composite, whatever form may have combined within them will either be (a) inclining towards one of the forms of the simples or not. If they do not so incline, they will be (b) either the result of the mean of the forms of the simples according to the degree of disproportion and deviation of the constituent from equality, or else (c) they will not be assimilated to any one of the simples, but will produce a form exceeding the requirement of the forms of the simples in both the measure of its simplicity or its complexity.

An example of the first type is the bitter taste when compounding aloe, a thing that is overpoweringly bitter, and honey, which is weakly sweet. An example of the second type is the color grey that holds an equal relationship to both of the extremes of blackness and whiteness that results on compounding a white and black opposite. An example of the third type is the stamp of a seal remaining in the clay that is composed of dry dust and liquid water being mixed together. It is known that the imprint in the clay does not meet the requirement of the forms of the simples whether one considers it in respect of the resulting compound or considered in respect of the simple things taken singly.

In other words, it is known that if the first type be made from simples whose forms oppose one another and not through the commingling but through blending such as an alloy or amalgam. In such cases, the contraries will be overpowered and will no longer exist on their own nor will they exist in the effects that are particular to them because it is impossible for two contraries to work together in one and the same medium. The utmost effect that they can exert will be to introduce a decrease in the strength of the overpower constituent and nothing more.

It is known in the second type in whatever proportions it be found that a reciprocity and equality both passive and active is imposed upon it. That is to say, the actions that the forms of the simples necessarily exert and the corresponding effects that these forms suffer mutually one from the other must of necessity be reciprocal, in the ratio of their respective proportions and strengths.

Lastly, it is known that the third type, if it comes to be, will not have resulted from the very self of the compound since it in no way belongs to it whether one considers it in either its simple or compound form. Therefore, it is not acquired from without.

Since these premises have been prefixed, we need to go deeper into our pursuit. We say that the soul has only come forth in compound bodies whose forms are opposite to each other and in none other. Its manifestation in them will not be divested or devoid of one of the three types.

However, it is not of the first division or else it would be heat or cold or dry or moist in whatever proportion one can conceive. How can one of these elemental qualities be fit to perform multiple powers given the fact that the decrease that occurred in its very composition and also what it would have expended in that decrease from its strength? No. How shall any one of these powers cause motion except towards one direction [i.e. heat rises, air rises, etc.] alone? It would be necessary to effect the displacement among psychical movements so that their mutual displacement. This would create a weariness.

It is not of the second type either since this is an impossibility. If the elements, however they be mixed in the proportion of powers, necessitates them to stop their effects. If the compound were left alone, it would never have to move. If it were to move upward, its heat would overpower the other elements. If it were to move downward, cold would overpower the other elements. It would not remain at rest in one of the four places in space where the four elemental qualities dwell. Nature would attract it to itself and overpower all the elements.

The body, then, would neither move nor stand still while every body that is surrounded by another body is either still or moving. This would be a contradiction and what leads to this contradiction is itself a contradiction. Therefore, saying that this is impossible is true (*reduction ad absurdum*).

The coming forth of the soul and combining with the body only occurs with the third type, that the soul comes from the outside, from without, which is what we wanted to show.

4. DETAILED STATEMENT CONCERNING THE POWERS OF THE PLANT SOUL AND MENTIONING THE NEED FOR EACH ONE OF THEM

Therefore, bodies that have souls, if considered from these bodies having the plant power, they have the gaining of nourishment in common, but differ in growth and reproduction. Among beings that take nourishment, there are those that do not grow such as a living individual who reaches full growth and, then, is at a standstill in regard to growth or has declined through withering. Yet every growing thing obtains nourishment.

There are living beings that take nourishment but do not reproduce other than through seeds that are not yet harvest-ripe or an animal that has not yet reached puberty. However, every thing that reproduces has to have passed through the state of taking in nourishment. The stage of reproduction, as well, will never be without the possibility of taking in nourishment.

In addition to having the taking-in of nourishment in common, they also have the possibility of growth in common. However, the way that they reproduce differs. There are animals that produce their own species not yet in the stage of puberty. However it be, they have passed through a period of growth and nutrition.

The plant soul, then, has three powers: nutritive, growth and reproduction.

Of these the nutritive is as the starting point; reproduction is the aim and end; and growth promoting as the mean binding the end to the starting-place. Indeed the ensouled body stands in absolute need of these three powers for the following reasons:

Whereas the Divine Command came down upon Nature enjoining upon it the task of forming a compound living being out of the four elements after such fashion as they are called for in it; and whereas Nature itself is unable to originate an ensouled body at one stroke, but can do so only by promoting its growth little by little; and whereas an individual that is put together after the manner of an animal is susceptible of being again decomposed and decaying by the nature of its constituents; and whereas a thing composed of opposites will not keep up so protracted a duration and last so long a time as is expected of it, therefore, Nature is in want of a power by which it can fabricate a living body by promotion of growth.

Nature has been supplied by Divine Providence with the growth giving potentiality; and is in want of a power whereby it can preserve the ensouled body at an even standard over against the waste which it undergoes in making up for what disintegration wears away from it. Therefore, it has been succored by Divine Providence with the nutritive power.

It is in want of a power that shall mold out of the living natural body a piece that it shall dwell in, in order that if corruption permeate the body, it shall have sought for itself a successor as a substitute whereby to arrive at the preservation of species. Nature has been helped by the Divine Providence with the reproductive power.

We have seen that growth follows nutrition and both of these by the reproduction power in erecting the living body and preserving it through its particular actions. Yet, it actually works in the opposite direction. First is to enthrall the material potentially to receive life through procreating as this power first clothes the material in a perfect form and then passes it to growth and then nutrition.

As soon as this is achieved, it keeps the form of the material within its three dimensions of length, breadth and thickness in its action of growth towards the end to which it strives. Growth then stops and the nutritive power enthralls the material.

The reproductive function is the one served, not the servant. In comparison to it, the nutritive function is the servant, not the one served. In the same way, the growth promoting function is served in one sense and serving in another.

The nutritive power, although it does not exist as the one served in the powers, yet it does occasionally employ the four sources of nature: attracting, retaining, digesting and repelling. That which is striven for in the process of making the form is only the bringing about of the perfection in matter in the shape proposed, not the bringing about of growth or nutrition. This is only that there is need for the growth and nutrition in order to realize the desired perfection and not the converse. So the final aim is the reproduction function to the exclusion of growth and nutrition.

And through God is fitness to be achieved.

5. Detailed Statement Concerning the Animal Powers and Mentioning the Need for Each One of Them

I affirm that every animal has sensation. It moves itself in some sort of motion at will. Every animal moves itself in some sort of motion at will and hence it has sensation. As sensation does not function to move itself at will and therefore, is wasted and useless in this regard, and the lack of it in what does move itself at will is harmful, Nature, owing to the Divine Providence that has been joined to it, gives nothing whatever that is either wasted or harmful, nor withholds either the necessary nor the useful.

Perhaps someone may object saying that shellfish are of such as have sensation and yet do not move themselves at will. This objection, however, will quickly vanish on experiment. Although shellfish do not move themselves from their places in a sort of organic locomotion at will, yet they do more or less shrink themselves up and spread out inside of their shells as I have witnessed with my own eyes on having tried the experiment more than once. I turned the shell over onto its back so that its position for drawing nourishment became separated from the ground. It ceased not to struggle until it had again stood in a position that made it easy for it to draw in nourishment from the muddy bottom.

And now that this has become certain for us, we shall further say: That whereas Divine Wisdom has decreed that an animal moving itself at will shall be composed of the four elements and as such animal would not be secure against the evils of mishaps in its successive change of places during movement, it has been fitted out with the sense of touch so as to flee through it from unfit places and seek those that are fit.

Any such animal's constitution cannot get on without

nourishment; and as its gaining its food is a sort of free will effort; and as some articles of food suit it and others not, it has been fitted out with the sense of taste. These two senses are both useful and necessary in life. The rest are useful, but not necessary.

After the tasting in degree of utmost need for it comes the sense of smell since odors will point the animal with a strong indication towards suitable articles of nourishment. Nor will the animal be at all able to get on without nourishment nor will its nourishment be obtained by it save through self-help. So Divine Providence has deemed fit to impart the sense of smell into most animals.

Next comes the sense of seeing. The how and why of its usefulness, as to the animal, which moves itself at will, is that whereas its betaking itself to certain spots, such as fire hearths, and away from certain spots (such as mountain peaks and seashores) that will lead to its hurt. Therefore Divine Providence has deemed fit to impart the sense of seeing into most animals.

Then comes the sense of hearing. The how and why of its usefulness is that things the harmful and useful may often be recognized as such, through it, by the peculiarity of their sounds and voices. Divine Providence has deemed fit to impart the sense of hearing into most animals. Moreover, the use made of this power by the rational species of the animal genus is of all three nearly the highest.

This then is an outline of the how and why of the uses of the five external senses.

And whereas trustworthy arrival at a knowledge of the mutually suitable and the mutually repellent will come about only through experiment or experience, Divine Providence has deemed fit to impart common sense into living animals in order that they shall through it collect the forms of things perceived by the senses. It also imparts the sense of retaining forms, in order that they shall through it preserve the meaning conceived out of things perceived by common sense.

It imparts the imaginative power in order that they shall through it restore what shall be wiped out from the memory by a sort of motion. It imparts the ability to sense an intention in order that they shall through it fix upon the sound (true) and the weak (false) of what the imagination extracts, namely to fix upon the true and false thereof with more or less the presumption of certainty, until the living beings shall review it in the mind.

As for the how and why the need for power of motivation, it is that whereas the position of the animal is not the same as the position of the plant in its adaptation for attracting such foods as are useful and pushing off such as are harmful and incompatible, but on the contrary as this is brought about for the animal through a sort of earning by self-help, it needs a moving power for the purpose of drawing to itself the useful and driving away the harmful.

Wherefore all the psychophysical powers of the animal are either part of perception or motivation, motivation promotes the yearning or longing or craving powers of attraction to pleasure (concupiscent, lust) and avoidance of harm/pain (irascible, anger). It is either urging on to the search after a chosen object of animal good and then it is the power of lust or else it is urging on to the warding off of an object of animal dislike and then it is the power of anger. The perceiving power, as well, is either external such as the five senses, or internal such as common sense, the retaining of forms, the imaginative, the ability to sense an intention (estimation), and memory.

Furthermore, the power of motivation does not cause to move save on a peremptory bidding from the internal sense of the ability to sense an intention through the means or by the use of the imaginative. Also, the power of motivation in animals, other than the rational species, is the aim and end. This is so, because the power of motivation is not imparted in them so that they will, through it, direct the actions of the external

25

senses and imagination in order to adapt these actions to the attainment of their own good. On the contrary, the power of the external senses and of imagination are imparted to the non-rational animal solely in order to direct aright through them the actions of motion and to adapt these actions to the good of the animal.

The rational species of living beings does the reverse because unto it was imparted the power of motivation solely in order that through this force it shall be fitted to set aright the rational self, i.e., the rational intelligent soul, not the other way around.

Thus, the power of motivation in the non-rational animal is, as it were, the prince commander that is served. The five external senses are as the spies that are sent forth. Common sense is the post-master of the prince commander unto whom the spies return to retain the forms. The imagining power is as the foot-messenger going to and fro between the post and the post-master. The ability to sense an intention is as the prince's adjutant minister. Memory is as the closet holding state papers.

As for the starry firmament and plants, sensation and the imagining power have not been imparted unto them, even though each one of them has a soul and though it has life: the firmament has not these powers, because of its loftiness; plants have them not because of their abasement in comparison to it.

6. DETAILED STATEMENT CONCERNING THE EXTERNAL SENSES AND HOW THEY PERCEIVE

As to the seeing power, philosophers have differed on the question of how they perceive. Thus one set among them asserts that they perceive solely through a ray that shoots out beyond the eye, and so encounters the sensible objects that are seen. This is Plato's way.

Others assert that the perceiving power itself encounters the sensible objects that are seen and so perceives them. Still others say that visual perception consists in this: When the intervening transparent body becomes effectively transparent by light shining upon it, then an impression of the outspread individual of such sensible objects as are seen is effected in the crystalline lens of the eye, just such a pictorial impression as is effected in mirrors. Indeed, the two effects are so similar that were mirrors possessed of a seeing power they would perceive the form imprinted in them. This is Aristotle's way. It is the sound reliable opinion.

That Plato's view is false, is quite clear. For, were it true that a ray goes out from the seat of sight and encounters sensible object, then sight would be in no need of light, but would on the contrary perceive in the dark, and would rather illuminate the air on its exit into the dark. Moreover such a ray will not fail of one of two modes: either it will subsist throughout the eye only, in which case Plato's opinion that it goes forth from the eye is wrong; or else it will subsist throughout a body other than the material of which the eye is composed; for it must inevitably have a vehicle to carry it, seeing that a ray is an accidental quality or mode, and furthermore seeing that that body which is other than the eye will not fail, in its turn, of being, either:

Firstly, sent out from the eye, in which case it will follow as a matter of course that the eye will not see all that is beneath the clear blue of the sky since one body will not penetrate throughout the whole of another body, unless forsooth it moves the latter away and occupies its place; and even should the disputer plead a vacuum, not only does Plato deny the existence of a vacuum utterly, but also if we accommodatingly yield this point and admit the existence of a vacuum, yet for all this the body that goes forth from the eye will penetrate throughout the body of water, for example, into such of its pores as are empty only, and not into the whole of the water's bulk; so that even according to this opinion it will necessarily so be that the eye will see only some places of all that is under water.

Secondly, that body which is other than the eye will not fail of being an intervening body intermediate between the seer and the seen, in which case the light which comes forth from the eye will subsist through it; nevertheless this opinion too is unsound, for the reason that every thing whatsoever is, in proximity to its source, so much the stronger, and in this respect light has not its equal; whence it follows as regards the object seen that, however closely and nearly it approaches to the eye, our perception will then be stronger; and thus if we do away with the intermediary body, the eye will still perceive the object felt by its sense of sight, and thus the intermediary which is the vehicle and carrier of light is no longer needed, save accidentally (by chance); and then too there is no need, in order to see, for an exit of light: this too is a falsehood. Wherefore Plato's opinion is worthless.

As for such as hold that the perceiver of the thing seen is the imaginative power itself through the imprinting of the image of the sensible object upon these render the absent on the same footing as the present, since in the imaginative power there may exist the image of a sensible object, notwithstanding the absence afterwards of the object that had been so felt: at which time however the living being so preserving that image will not be qualified with sight but with imagination and memory.

Furthermore these theorists make a greater blunder still, seeing that they render a thing of Nature's make and composition wholly idle, useless, and needed in the operation of visual perception; inasmuch as in their opinion the imaginative power itself meets immediately sensible objects, and thus spares Nature the task of adapting an organ, to wit the complex eye.

Wherefore the sound theory is that the configurations of things stand out in the transparent ambient if it be effectively transparent on the shinning of a luminant upon it and hence they do not appear but in a polished body capable of receiving them such as mirrors and the like; and so too there is in the eye a crystalline lens into which the images of things are imprinted, just as their impression into mirrors; and in it, i.e., the lens or the eye, has been fitted up the seeing power so that, if such forms are imprinted in it, it perceives them. Moreover, the objects of perception belonging in truth and deed to sight are the colors.

As for the hearing power: it hears only sound and sound is a motion of air that the ear feels on two hard smooth bodies coming quickly close up one to the other, the escaping of the air from between them, its striking the ear, and its moving the air that is kept ready within the organ of hearing.

Thus, if this inside air move the organ and if this organ's motion act upon the nerve of hearing, the sense of hearing perceives it in the measure of the strength or weakness of that motion. Indeed, hardness is a condition without which it could not be, for, in the case of two soft bodies, the air will not escape from them, but will dissipate itself throughout their pores. Smoothness too is just such a condition; because, in the case of unsmooth bodies, not the whole of the air will escape from between them suddenly and violently, but will be shut up in the passages. And rapidity of contact also is a like condition; for if it come about gently and slowly, the air would not escape violently.

29

Tho echo too will arise from the rebound of the air escaping from between the two encountering bodies by reason of its hitting against another hard flat or hollow body filled with air, because of the air that is within it hindering the penetration of the escaped air, and the latter's striking the ear again after the first stroke, on the same wise as in the first instance.

As to the smelling power; it smells odors in the sniffing in of air that has received its odor from an odoriferous body, as one body receives its warmth from another warm body. Thus, if an animal snuffs up air like this into its nose until such air touches the front of the brain, and alters it to its own odor, the smelling power feels it.

As for taste, it arises only on the coming to pass of the following change: when the moisture of the tasting organ, to wit the tongue, becomes transformed into the juice of the newly-come food; and when the mass or this organ has received that juice, the tasting power will perceive what has happened within the instrument.

As for touch: it will only arise upon the organ's receiving the quality of that which is touched, and upon the touching power's perceiving what has been thus presented within the organ.

Furthermore, simple sensibles, that are at once primary and as such the bases of all others, are in pairs, of which there are eight; and if we make each into singles, they become sixteen, to wit: Touch, four pairs: 1. heat and cold; 2. moisture and dryness; 3. roughness and smoothness; 4. hardness and softness. The four remaining senses, each having a pair, that is, smelling, one pair, which is fragrant odor and fetid stinking odor; tasting, one pair, that is, sweet and bitter; hearing, one pair, namely, heavy sound and dull and shrill; sight, one pair, to wit, white and black.

All other sensibles are made up from these simples, and are intermediates between some two of them, as for example grey from white and black; lukewarm from hot and cold. Moreover all sensibles are felt wholly and solely through a sort of gathering and sundering, shrinking and spreading except sounds, which are felt only through splitting apart. Thus:

1. Warmth is felt through splitting apart
2. Cold is felt through gathering
3. Moisture through spreading
4. Dryness through shrinking
5. Roughness through splitting apart
6. Smoothness through spreading
7. Hardness through repelling, which is a sort of gathering and shrinking
8. Softness through being repelled, which is not devoid of spreading and splitting apart
9. Sweetness through spreading, devoid of splitting apart
10. Bitterness through splitting apart and shrinking
11. Fragrant odor through spreading, devoid of splitting apart
12. Stinking odor through splitting apart and shrinking
13. Whiteness through splitting apart
14. Blackness through gathering
15. and 16. Sounds such as heavy sound and dull and shrill

As to the intermediaries between the feeling powers and the felt forms, they are themselves devoid of the forms of sensibles. Otherwise it would not be possible for them to be intermediaries since their own forms, if they had any, would then so engage the opposite power as to divert it from perceiving any other forms. Such voidness or freedom from forms is either totally and altogether void, or else relatively void through equableness of the forms in the intermediaries, such as the equable proportion of the qualities touched in meat, which is a medium between the touching power and the quality touched, although meat is incontestably made up of qualities that are touched. Yet, notwithstanding this, the

31

equableness of the qualities has annihilated the forms in it.

Examples of the first division—absolute void and freedom from form—are the freedom of air, of water, and of what resembles them among the various intermediaries of sight, from color; the freedom of air and of water, both which are the two mediums of smelling, from odor; the freedom of water, which is the medium of tasting, from flavor; and the steadiness of the air, which is the medium of hearing, and its freedom from motion.

Further, each of these powers, to wit the five senses, if actually functioning, perceives only through coming into relation with the object felt. Nay, rather it only perceives at first so much as has been traced in it of the form of the object felt. Thus, the eye only perceives that form which has imprinted itself in it of the object felt so also the remainder of the senses.

Again, in the case of strong wearying sensibles such as a loud noise, a strong smell, a shining and a flashing light, if they are repeated upon the organ, spoil and dullen it through their overworking it.

Again, each one of the five senses perceives, through the means of its own rightful perception and besides the same, five other things, to wit: 1. shape; 2. number; 3. size; 4. motion; 5. rest (quiet). That sight, touch, and taste perceive them, is evident.

As to hearing, it perceives, in accordance with the variety of the number of sounds, the number of the sound-emitting objects; and, through the strength of the sounds. It perceives the size of the two objects that are hitting against each other and, in accordance with a kind of change and fixedness of the sounds, it perceives motion and rest. In accordance with their volume around the sound-emitter, be the latter solid or hollow, it perceives some sorts of shapes.

As to smelling, it knows, in accordance with the change of directions whence the odors are emitted and reach it, and through the variety of these odors in their qualities. I say it knows the number of the things smelt through the measure of abundance of the smells, the size of such things; through the measure of proximity and distance, changeableness and fixedness.

It recognizes their motion and their rest. In accordance with the sides on which their odor reaches it from one and the same body, it knows their shape. Still, these discriminations are very weak in this power among humanity, owing to the weakness of the power itself in the human race. For all this, people have not the keen scent that many other animals have, and therefore such discriminations are very weak in people.

7. DETAILED STATEMENT CONCERNING THE INTERNAL SENSES

Not one of the outward senses unites within itself the perception of color, odor, and softness and yet, we often come upon a body that is yellow, and perceive at once so much about it, namely that it is honey, sweet, nice of smell, and fluid, although we have neither tasted, nor smelt, nor even touched it. It is clear that we possess a power wherein are assembled the perceptions of the four senses, and have thus become summed up in it into one single form. Were it not for this power, we should not know that sweetness, for instance, is other than blackness, since the discriminator between two things is he who has known them both.

This is the power which is designated as the common sense. And were it one of the outward apparent senses, its sway would limit itself to the state of wakefulness only. Yet, ocular observation attests what is quite otherwise. This sense does at times perform its action in both the states of sleep and wakefulness.

Furthermore, there is in animals a sense that sets up such forms as have assembled all the common sense, discriminates between them and differentiates them without the forms themselves disappearing from the common sense. And this sense is undoubtedly other than the power of the retention of forms. In the latter there are none but real forms that have been obtained from sense whereas in this case it may be otherwise.

It may imagine and picture wrongly and falsely, and what it had not received after such a wrong and false shape from any one of the senses. This sense is the one named imagination.

Further, there is in animals a power (estimation) that passes judgment, upon such or such a thing that it is so or not so. It does this decisively. As a result, the animal flees away from shunned evil and seeks chosen good. It is also evident that this

35

sense is other than the imaginative, since this last imagines images of the sun in accordance with what it has obtained from the opposite sense, to be of the size of its disc and so forth.

The matter stands in this sense quite otherwise. So, too, the lion finds its prey from far away, even the size of a small bird, yet its form and size in no way perplex it, but it makes for it. It is also evident that this sense is other than the imaginative. This is because the imaginative power performs its manifold deeds without belief and conviction on its part that matters are in accordance with its imagining. This power is what is named the estimative or the surmising faculty or judgment, the ability to sense an intention.

Further, there is in living beings a sense that preserves the purports (or thoughts and conceptions) of what the senses had perceived, such as, for instance, that the wolf is an enemy or the child, a beloved next of kin. Wherefore, so much at least if not more is evident, that this sense is other than the common sense inasmuch as in the latter there are no forms but such as it has gained from the senses. Again, the senses did not feel the wolf's enmity, nor the child's love, but alone the wolf's image, and the child's bodily shape.

As to love and fierceness, it is the mind's eye alone that has obtained them and then stored them up in this power. It is also clear that this power is other than the imaginative power for the reason that this last does at times imagine what is other than that which the mind's eye has deemed right, found true, and has derived from the senses. The former power, that is, the one here dealt with, imagines none other than what the mind's eye has deemed right, has found true, and derived from the senses.

This power is also other than the ability to sense an intention or sense of surmising for the reason that this last does not preserve what some other has deemed to be true, but it of its own self deems to be true, whilst the power here treated of does not itself pass judgment of truth or falsehood, but only preserves what another has deemed to be true. This power is called memory, the preserving or keeping sense.

Again, the imaginative power is called by this name—imagination—if the ability to sense an intention or surmising sense alone uses it. If the rational soul uses it, it is called the thinking or cogitative sense.

The heart is the source of all these senses or powers in Aristotle's opinion. The sway over them, however, is in different organs. Thus the sway over the external senses is in their known organs whereas the sway over the common sense is in the anterior hollow (ventricle) of the brain. The sway over the imaginative, in the middle hollow thereof. The sway over memory is in the posterior hollow thereof. The sway over the ability to sense an intention or surmising is throughout all the brain, but above all in the compartment of the imagination within the brain [or, throughout the whole of the brain, but more especially alongside of the imaginative thereof].

And in so far as these hollows or ventricles suffer harm and hurt, so will the manifold actions of these senses suffer as well. Were the senses standing independently, that is to say subsisting in themselves, and efficient independently, that is to say putting forth their actions of themselves, they would not need, for their proper and peculiar actions, any sort of organ.

One recognizes in this way that their senses do not subsist in themselves, but that the undying power is the rational soul, as we shall hereafter set forth. Yet for all this, the soul does maybe at times seek out for itself so to speak the purest quintessence of the kernels of these senses and cause them to exist of themselves, the setting forth of which shall soon follow.

8. ON THE HUMAN SOUL FROM THE BEGINNING TO ITS PERFECTION

No doubt that the rational species of the genus animal is distinguished from the non-rational by a power, through which it is enabled to imagine things rational. This is called the rational soul. The custom has obtained of calling it the mind, that is to say the potential mind, thus likening it to matter which is potential matter. Moreover this power is found in the whole human species. It possesses in itself at the outset none of the mentally grasped forms, but these arise within it after two sorts of processes.

The first is through a Divine Guidance, without effort of study, and without profitting from the senses. An example is the mentally grasped self-evident axioms like our conviction that the whole is greater than the part and that two contradictories do not come together at one time in one and the same thing. The sane-minded adults share equally in the acquisition of such forms.

The second sort of process is through earning [the mental thought or truth] by the reasoning process and by an array of proof and demonstration such as the conception of logical truths, like genera, species, differences; and properties, simple terms, and terms compounded in the various ideas into one composite term; justly worded syllogisms, both valid and false; propositions which if put into syllogisms lead to necessary demonstrated results, or to argumentative probable results, or to equally balanced rhetorical results, or to axiomatical sophistical results, or to impossible poetical results.

Such mentally grasped forms as the recognition of the certainty of natural realities such as primary matter and form; non-existence and Nature; place and time; rest and motion; bulky bodies of the sky—firmament and bulky elemental bodies; absolute universal being and absolute nothingness; generation absolute and corruption; absolute origin of things generated that are within the sky; that are within the deepest depths of mines; that are on the earth's crust amongst which last named are plant and animal; the true conception. of the human being and the truth of the soul's conception of its own self.

Still further, such mentally grasped forms as the conception of idea; mathematics amongst which are number, pure geometry, stellar geometry, harmonical or musical geometry, optical geometry. Agan, farther still, such ideas as the conception of divine affairs such as the knowledge of the principles of the absolute Self-Existent in so far as he exists pcr se; and of the principles consequently adhering to Him such as potentiality, power and efficiency, first cause and accounting cause, essence and accidents, genus and species, incompatibility and homogeneity, agreement and disagreement, unity and multiplicity.

Still further, the fixing of the principles of the theoretical sciences amongst which are the mathematical, the natural and the logical—all which cannot be attained save through this latter science. Still further, such as proving the first Creator and the first Created; the Universal Soul and how creation came about; the relative position of the mind towards creation; the relative position of soul towards the mind; the relative position of matter towards nature; of forms towards the soul; the relative position of the skies, orbs, planets and all existing things towards matter and towards form; why and wherefore they differ so widely as they do as to forwards and backwards of development; and the knowledge of the divine government, universal nature, primal providence, prophetic inspiration, the Divine Spirit, sublime angels, attaining to the certainty of the Creator's being beyond all partnership and similitude [i.e. recognizing the truth that polytheism and anthropomorphism are to be rejected]; attaining to the knowledge of what rewards await the righteous and what punishments impend the wicked; or the delight and the pain overtaking souls after their abandoning the bodies.

Further, this power that conceives these ideas does at

times gain from sense, forms mental, imaginative, and innate or instinctive to itself.

In such a case it does this in that it lays before itself the forms that are in the conceiving sense and in the remembering sense by employing the imaginative and the ability to sense an intention or surmise, and then contemplates them, and finds them to have participated in some forms and to have differed in some other forms. It finds some amongst the forms that are in these senses to be essential and others to be accidental.

And as to their participation in forms, it is like the participation of a form in the conceiver's mind; in the idea of life; and the differing of the two in the idea of the rational and non-rational.

As to the essential form, it is like the life that is in them both; as for the accidental, it is like their blackness and whiteness. So that if we and the two aforesaid on this wise as stated, the mind makes each one of these essential and accidental, participated and peculiar forms, one universal mental form singly and alone, and thus through this working over process, it gets at mental genera, species, differences, properties, and accidents.

Then it combines these single notions into particular combinations; then into syllogistic argumentative combinations and deduces from them corollaries from the results — all which it gets through the service of the animal powers with the help of universal mind, after the manner that we shall set forth later on and through the intermediary of such necessary self-evident mental axioms as it has been endowed with.

Moreover this power, although it derives help from sensation when getting out single mental forms from the sensuous forms, yet it does not need the sensuous power for conceiving these ideas within itself and for setting up syllogisms out of them, neither when affirming, nor when conceiving the two dicta of abstraction and generalization, as we shall afterwards explain.

And to whatever extent it derives sensuous corollaries, for which there shall be need through the said working over process, yet it dispenses with the employment of sensation. It is even sufficient for and in itself for the carrying on of all its manifold activities. And just as sensation perceive solely through an assimilation of that which is felt, so also do the mental powers perceive solely through an assimilation of the mentally grasped. This assimilation is the abstraction of the form from matter and the adhering to it.

Sensation does not get a physical form through willed motion and voluntary action on its part, but through the arrival of the very thing felt unto it, either by chance or through the intermediary of motivation and abstraction with the help of the intermediaries that connect the forms with it.

In the case of reason, or understanding this process is otherwise. By and through itself it at times does itself perform the abstraction of form from matter as often as it wills and then clings unto it. And for this reason it is said that sensation is more or less passive in its conception [or, that sensation is after a fashion acted upon when it conceives], and that reasoning is active. Nay, rather it is said, for this reason that sensation cannot do without organs, and has in itself no efficiency. How is it possible to apply such a statement to reasoning?

The mind and the ability to understand or reason is, in fact, solely nothing other than the forms of mentally grasped things whether these be arrayed in the very mind potentially and through it they are brought out to effective action. Therefore, it is said that the mind is in fact and deed at once both understanding and understood.

Among the properties of understanding is the fact that it unifies the many and multiplies the one through analysis and synthesis. As to multiplication, it is such as the analysis of one person into essence, body, nourishment getting, animal, rational. As to unification of the many, it is such as the synthesis of this one person out of essence, body, animal, rational into one notion which is humanity.

Moreover the mind, although it applies its activity within a duration of time in arranging syllogisms through using reflection, yet the result itself, which this reflection obtains and which is the fruit of thought and the end sought after, is not dependant upon time, nor is it obtained save at an instant. Nay, more than this, the mind itself is solely above and beyond all time.

And the rational soul, if it engages itself upon the sciences, its activity is called intellect, and it is accordingly called theoretical intellect. And if it engages itself upon overcoming blameworthy powers that entice unto wrongdoing through their excess, into folly through their abandonment, into impetuosity and impulsivity through their agitation, into cowardice through their indifference or lukewarmness, or into wickedness through their excitement, or into degeneration through their smouldering, and leads them over into the paths of wisdom, courage, temperance, in short, unto God-consciousness, then its activity is called ruling or governing. Accordingly, it is called practical intellect or reason.

Again, the rational soul is sometimes so fitted out in a few persons through vigils and conjunction with the universal mind to be quite independent of taking refuge in syllogistic argument and reflection, but rather is sufficiently stored with inspiration and revelation to render it wholly absolved from such ordinary means as mental ratiocination. This peculiar property of the reasoning mind is called the sacred soul and it is accordingly called the Spirit. Unto such a favored rank and degree none shall attain save prophets upon whom be peace and blessing.

9. ESTABLISHING THE PROOFS NECESSARY FOR AFFIRMING THE RATIONAL SOUL

Let us begin with premises in order to establish the logical proofs for this claim.

First Premise: that the human being conceives universal ideas wherein a greater or less multitude participates such as the human being at large and animal at large. And of these universal ideas there are such as he conceives through a particular synthesis. There are such others of these universal ideas as he does not conceive by any synthesis, but singly and individually. And unless he shall have conceived the latter division, it is not possible for him to conceive the former.

Further, he conceives each one of these universal ideas only under one form, abstracted from all relationship to its concrete sensuous particulars since the particulars of each one of the universal ideas are potentially endless in variety and number. No one of the particulars has any right of priority over another particular in respect of that one form of the universal idea.

Second Premise: that a perfection, whatsoever body it detaches, reduces, and adorns, and, in general, whatsoever individual of divisible things it so takes hold of, it clothes the same and exactly fits the same in every one of its parts. And whatsoever clothes exactly fits a divisible thing in all its parts is itself divisible. Therefore, every form that has clothed and exactly fitted any body whatsoever is itself divisible.

Third Premise: that in every universal form, if regard be had in the division of such form, purely and simply to its abstract self, then it will not at all validly follow that the parts into which it has been divided shall necessarily resemble the whole in its complete notion. Otherwise it must follow that the universal form, whose division has been made in respect of its abstract self, has not been itself divided, but that it has been divided into its constituents whether these be its various species or its numerous individuals.

However, the multiplicity of species or of individuals does not necessarily entail division in the abstract universal idea itself. But it has been laid down as a fact that such division has actually taken place, which is a contradiction. Hence our assertion that the parts of the universal form do not resemble it in its full and complete notion is a true dictum.

Fourth Premise: that in the mental form, if regard be had to its division, it will not validly follow that its parts are stripped of the totality of its idea. This is so because if we admit such total stripping and assert that these parts are utterly aloof from the complete conception of the universal whole, then the form will arise in such parts only upon their assembling together so that they are in fact things devoid of that form which will arise in them on their being set together which is a quality of the parts of passive matter which occupies space.

Therefore, the division has not been effected in the universal form, but in its objective concrete materials. But it has been asserted that the division has come to pass in it: this too is a contradiction. Therefore, our assertion: It will not validly follow that its parts are stripped of the totality of its notion is a true statement.

Fifth Premise: which is the result of the two preceding: that in the universal form, if it be possible that divisibility be considered in it, then its parts are neither completely devoid of the perfect form nor are they completely exhaustive of it. They are, as it were, component, or constituent parts of its definition and description.

Given, then, these premises, we shall further unquestionably say that a mentally grasped form, in short, all knowledge, claims some abode somewhere. Its abode is both an essence itself and a part of the human self so that such essence will not be devoid of being either a divisible material body or a non-material, indivisible essence.

I say, however, that it is not permissible that it be a physical body because a universally mentally grasped form, if it abide in a body, then it is inevitably possible for divisibility to befall it as we have shown above.

Nor is it permissible that its parts be otherwise than resembling the whole from one stand point and contrasting with it from another. In a word, each one of the parts contains somewhat of the idea of the whole whereas there is no universal form whatsoever out of whose parts a compound can be formed that is partly like it and partly unlike it save genera and differences. Consequently these parts are genera and differences. Therefore, each one of them is in its turn a universal form.

Thus, the same assertion repeats itself as above. Inevitably this will end in a form that is no longer divisible into genus and differences owing to the impracticability of progression *ad infinitum* into parts differing in ideas, even if it be established that physical bodies are so divided into parts *ad infinitum*.

Moreover it is well-known that the universal form, concerning which it is held that it is divisible only into geneus and differences, if there be nevertheless some of these two that is not divisible into genera and differentia, then this some will be in itself utterly indivisible in every sense and respect.

Consequently, of what is compounded of these two, some will also be indivisible seeing that it is well-known, for example, that the human being cannot be conceived except along with the two conceptions living and rational. In short, it is not possible to conceive a universal form that has genus and differences except by conceiving them all together.

Therefore, the form which we have described as having taken up its abode in the body has not taken up its abode therein. This is a contradiction and therefore the diametrically contrary to it is true, namely our assertion that a uni-

versal mental idea does not abide in any physical body whatsoever. Consequently, the essence in which a generic mental
form abides is spiritual essence, not qualified with the qualities of bodies, which is what we call the rational soul. And
this is what we set out to show.

A second of the proofs which corroborate this claim
and confirm it, is what I am now going to set forth. I say,
then, that body of and through itself does not effect conception of mentally grasped things since all bodies have in
common that they are body and differ amongst each other
in capacity for conceiving mentally grasped things.

Living bodies are qualified to conceive mentally
grasped things only by and through certain powers that
are put within them. If these powers conceive by and
through themselves without the cooperation of the body, it
follows that they are in themselves fit and apt to be an abode
for mental form. What is thus qualified is itself an essence.
Therefore, if such conception is occurring, they, namely,
these powers, are essences.

Now, it is clear that this power conceives mentally
grasped things by and through itself only and not at all
through cooperation of the body. We contend, concerning
whatsoever perceives anything through cooperation of body,
that the oftener wearying perceptibles are repeated upon it
the more do they tend towards ruining and spoiling it and
producing dullness and exhaustion in it, it being nothing but
a frail organ whose strength has been reduced owing to the
over-tasking imposed upon it by the power's employing it.
In this cause, the sense of seeing, for example, gets weaker
the oftener it persists in looking at the sun's shape. So, too,
the sense of hearing, if loud sounds reach it repeatedly.

Whereas this rational soul, that is, the one that conceives
mentally grasped things, the more it perceives wearying mental conceptions, the stronger it becomes for its work [the

more efficient it becomes]. Wherefore it has no need for an organ in its operation of perceiving. Therefore, it perceives of itself. Now, we have already shown that every soul perceiving of its own self is an essence. So, then, this power is an essence, which is what we set out to show.

Among the proof that guide to this claim is what I shall now show, so I say as follows:

The immanence of form in body is at once both passive and receptive—passivity of the form and receptivity of the body. And whereas one and the some thing excludes the possibility of its being both doer and done, it becomes clear unto us that a body is not able of itself to dress itself in one mentally grasped form and strip off another.

Yet nevertheless we see a person consciously and with forethought conceiving and proceeding from one mentally grasped form to another. This operation is not devoid of being either an act peculiar to body, or else an act peculiar to the rational soul or finally an act commonly shared between them both. It is not permissible to attribute action and doing peculiarly and specially to body. Nay. I will say and not even to body conjointly with the rational soul since body is a coadjutor of that force or power, helping towards affording an abode for any form whatsoever in that body's own self.

Since it has become known to us that body along with the soul will both become fit subjects for this form that has thus arisen, a subject, however, is to be stigmatized with nothing beyond simple passivity alone. Here, both these two are aggressive acts and deeds. Therefore, this is an act peculiar to the soul. And everything that is in it that emanates from its own self has had no need for another thing to help it. It will not need in its own structure anything beyond its own self to help it seeing that independence or isolation in the structure of self precedes independence or isolation in the putting forth of self-emanating action.

Therefore, this power is an essence standing of itself, independent of body. Therefore, the rational soul is an essence.

Among the proofs that point to the validity of this contention is what I am now going to say. No doubt a living body and living organs, if they accomplish their growing age and the age of no longer growing, begin to wither and diminish, to lose power and waste away. This in human beings is on passing forty years.

Now, were the rational reasoning soul organic, then there would be found not one single individual of humanity at these years of his age but what this power of his would have begun to diminish. However, the case in most people is quite otherwise. Indeed, it is usual amongst the majority that as to intellectual power they improve in cleverness and increase in insight. Therefore, the structure of the rational soul is not upheld by the body nor by the organ. This power is an essence standing of itself which is what we wished to show.

Among the proofs for the validity of this contention is the following also. So much at least is clear, namely, that not one of the bodily powers has the strength for performing infinite multifarious actions. This is so because the strength of the one half of such a body will inevitably be found to be weaker than the strength of the whole.

The weaker is less powerful to perform and overcome than the stronger. Whatsoever, other than the infinite, receives less is itself finite. Therefore, the strength of each one of the two halves is finite. Too, their, sum is finite since the sum of two finites is itself finite. As it has been contended that it is infinite, this is a contradiction.

Therefore, the sound view is that the powers are not powerful enough to perform infinite manifold deeds. The rational soul, however, is powerful enough to perform many infinite deeds seeing that forms geometrical, arithmetical, and philosophical, which the rational soul has to perform among other of its acts, are infinite. Therefore the rational soul is not standing by and through the body. Therefore, it stands of itself and is an essence of itself. Further, so much at least is clear that the corruption of one of two conjoined essences does not entail and enjoin the corruption of the other wherefore the death of the body does not render obligatory the death of the soul, which is what we wanted to show.

10. Establishing the Argument for the Existence of the Active Intellect

As to the mental essence, we find it in infants devoid of every mental form. Then, later on in life we find in it self-evident axiomatic mentally grasped ideas without effort of learning and without reflection. So that the arising of them within it will not fail to be either through sense and experience, or else through divine outpouring reaching to it.

But it is not permissible to hold that the arising of such primary mental form will be through experience, seeing that experience does not afford and supply necessary and inevitable judgment. Experience does not go so far as to believe or disbelieve definitively the existence of something different to the judgment drawn from what it has perceived.

Indeed experience, although it shows us that every animal we perceive moves on chewing the lower jaw, yet it does not supply us with convincing judgment that such is the case with every animal; for were this true, it would not be permissible for the crocodile to exist which moves his upper jaw on chewing.

Therefore not every judgment we have arrived at, as to things through our perception is applicable to and holds good of all that we have perceived or have not perceived of such thing. However, it may so be that what we have not perceived differs from what we have perceived.

Whereas our conception that a whole is greater than a part is not formed because we have sensuously felt every part and every whole that are so related, seeing that even such an experience will not guarantee to us that there will be no whole and no part differently related.

The same is true of the dictum concerning the impossibility of two opposites coming together in one and the same thing and that things which are equal to one and the same thing are equal to one another. And likewise the dictum concerning our holding proofs to be true if they be valid, (or the belief in and conviction of their validity does not become valid by and through learning and effort of study or else this would draw out *ad infinitum* [inasmuch as each proof rests upon given presuppositions, whose validity would in its turn have to be proved]. Nor is this gained from sense for the reason that we have mentioned.

Consequently both the latter as well as the former certainty are gained from a Divine outflow reaching to the rational soul and the rational soul reaching unto it so that this mental idea arises therein. Also, as to this outflow, unless it have in its own self such a universal mental form, it would not be able to engrave it within the rational soul. Hence such form is in the outflow's own self. And whatsoever self has in it a mental form is an essence, other than a body, and not within a body, and standing of itself.

Therefore this outflow unto which the soul reaches is a mental essence, not a body, not in a body, standing of itself, and one which stands towards the rational soul in the stead of light to sight. Yet, however, with this difference, namely that light supplies to sight the power of perceiving only and not the perceived form whereas this essence supplies exclusively by and through its sole and single self to the rational power, the power of perceiving. It brings about therein the perceived forms as well, as we have set forth above.

Now, if the rational soul's conceiving rational forms be a source of completion and perfection for it and be effected and brought about on reaching to this essence and if worldly earthly labors, such as its thought, its sorrows, and joy, its longings, hamper the power and withhold it from reaching there, so that it will not reach there except through abandoning the powers and getting rid of them, there being nothing to stop it from continued reaching save the living body, then consequently if it quit the body it will not cease to be reaching to its Perfector and attached to Him.

Again, what reaches to its Perfector and attaches itself to

54

Him is safe against corruption, all the more so if even during disconnection from Him it has not undergone corruption. Therefore, the rational soul after death shall ever remain and continue unwavering [and undying]. Attached to this noble essence, which is called the universal intellect, and in the language of the lawgivers, Divine Knowledge.

As to the other powers, such as the animal and the vegetable: Whereas every one of them performs its proper peculiar action only by and through the living body and in no other way, consequently they will never quit living bodies, but will die with their death seeing that everything which is and yet has no action, is idle and useless.

Yet nevertheless the rational soul does gain, by its connection with them, from them their choicest and purest lye and wash, and leaves for death the husks. And were it not so, the rational soul would not use them in consciousness. Wherefore the rational soul shall surely depart taking along the kernels of the other powers after death ensues.

We have thus made a clear statement concerning souls and which souls are everlasting, and which of them will not be fitted out and armed with everlastingness. It still remains for us, in connection with this research, to show how a soul exists within living bodies and the aim and end for which it is found within the same and what measure will be bestowed upon it in the hereafter of eternal delight and perpetual punishment and of temporary punishment that ceases after a duration of time that shall ensue upon the decease of the living body and to treat of the idea that is designated by the lawgivers as intercession and of the quality of the four angels and the throne bearer.

Were it not however that the custom prevails to isolate such research from the research whose path we have been treading, out of high esteem and reverence for it, and to make the latter research precede in order of treatment of the former, to the end of levelling the road and paving it solidly, I should have followed up these ten sections with a full and complete treatment of the subject dealt with in them. Notwithstanding all this, were it not for fear of wearying by verbosity, I would have disregarded the demands of custom herein.

Thus, then, whatever it may please the Prince—God prolong his highness—to command as to treating singly of such ideas, I shall put forth, in humble compliance and obedience, my utmost effort, God Almighty willing.

May wisdom never cease to revive through him to flourish after withering so that its sway may be renewed through his sway. May through his days, its days come back again and through his prestige, the prestige of its devotees be exalted and the seekers after its favor abound, so God almighty will.

57

BIBLIOGRAPHY

PRIMARY SOURCES

Avicenna. (1906). *Qasida al-Ainiyya* (*Ode to the Soul*) II, pp. 110-111. Translated by E. G. Browne. *A Literary History of Persia* 4 vols. London: T. Fisher Unwin.

———(1326/1908). *Rasail Fi Ilm al-Akhlaq* in *Tis Rasail fi al-Hikmah wa al-Tabiyyat*. Cairo: Amin Hindiyyah.

———(1326/1908). *Tis Rasail Fil-Hikmah wal-Tabiyyat*. Cairo: Amin Hindiyyah.

———1326/1908). *Rasail Fil-Ahd* in *Tis Rasail Fil-Hikmah wal-Tabiyyat*. Cairo: Amin Hindiyyah.

———(1930). *Qanun fil Tibb: A Treatise on the Canon of Medicine by Avicenna, Incorporating a Translation of the First Book*. Translated by O. Cameron Gruner. London, UK: Luzac & Co.

———(1936). *Kitab al-Najat*. 2d ed. Cairo: Muhy al-Din Sabri al-Kurdi.

———(1951). *On Theology*. Translated by Arthur J. Arberry. CT: Hyperion Press.

———(1331-1951). *Risalah dar Haqiqat wa Kaifiyat-i Silsila-yi Mawjudat wa Tasalsul-i Asbab wa Musabbabat*. Edited by Musa Amid. Tehran: Anjuman-i-Athar-i Milli.

———(1331/1952). *Danishnamah-yi Ala al-Dawlah* (Book of Science Dedicated to Ala al-Dawlah), *Ilahiyat*. Edited by Muhammad Moin. Tehran: Anjuman-i Athar-i Milli.

———(1952). *Ahwal al-Nafs*. Edited by Ahmad Fuad al-Ahwani. Cairo: Isa al-babi al-Halabi.

———(1952). *Kitab al-Najat: Avicenna's Psychology: An English Translation of Kitab al-Najat, Book II, Chapter VI with Historico-Philosophical Notes and Textual Improvements on the Cairo Edition*. (FR) Translated by Fazlur Rahman. Oxford, UK: Oxford University Press.

———(1954). *Fil-Akhlaq wal-Infialat al-Nafsaniyyah*. Cairo: Publications de l'Institut Francais d'Archeologie Oriental.

———(1958). *Kitab al-Isharat wal-Tanbihat*. Edited by Sulayman Dunya. 4 parts in 3 vols. Cairo: Dar al-Maarif.

———(1959). *Kitab al-Nafs* in *Kitab al-Shifa: Physics VI*. Edited by F. Rahman. London: Oxford University Press.

———(1973). *Metaphysics* in *Kitab al-Shifa*. Translated by Parviz Morewedge. London: Routledge & Kegan Paul.

———(1982). *Kitab al-Isharat wal-Tanbihat*. Edited by J. Forget. Leiden: E. J. Brill.

———(1997). *Qanun fil-Tibb* (*The Canon of Medicine*) (*TCM*), vol. 1. Adapted by Laleh Bakhtiar from the translations of O. Cameron Gruner and Mazar H. Shah. Great Books of the Islamic World. Chicago, IL: KAZI Publications.

———(2005) *Kitab al-Shifa, Kitab al-Ilahiyat* (*Metaphysics of the Healing*). Translated by Michael E. Marmura with Arabic Edition. Provo, UT: Brigham

Young University Press.

————(2009). *Kitab al-Shifa, al-Tabiiyat*, as *Sama al-Tabii* (*Physics of the Healing*). Translated by Jon McGinnis with Arabic edition. Provo: Brigham Young University Press.

————(2012) *Qanun fil-Tibb* (*The Canon of Medicine: Natural Pharmaceuticals*), vol. 2. Compiled by Laleh Bakhtiar. Great Books of the Islamic World. Chicago, IL: KAZI Publications.

————(2012) *Qanun fil-Tibb* (*The Canon of Medicine*: *Natural Pharmaceuticals*, vol. 2, *On Cosmetics and their Medicinal Uses*). Compiled by Laleh Bakhtiar. Great Books of the Islamic World. Chicago, IL: KAZI Publications.

————(2012) *Qanun fil-Tibb* (*The Canon of Medicine*) (*TCM*), vol. 1, *On Diagnosis: Signs and Symptoms*. Adapted by Laleh Bakhtiar from translations by O. Cameron and Mazar H. Shah. Great Books of the Islamic World. Chicago, IL: KAZI Publications.

————(2012) *Qanun fil-Tibb* (*The Canon of Medicine*) (*TCM*), vol. 1, *On Diseases, Causes and Symptoms*. Adapted by Laleh Bakhtiar from translations by O. Cameron and Mazar H. Shah. Great Books of the Islamic World. Chicago, IL: KAZI Publications.

————(2012) *Qanun fil-Tibb* (*The Canon of Medicine*) (*TCM*), vol. 1, *On Healthy Living: Childbirth and Infancy*. Adapted by Laleh Bakhtiar from translations by O. Cameron and Mazar H. Shah. Great Books of the Islamic World. Chicago, IL: KAZI Publications.

————(2012) *Qanun fil-Tibb* (*The Canon of Medicine*) (*TCM*), vol. 1, *On Healthy Living: Exercising, Massaging, Bathing, Eating, Drinking, Sleeping and Treating Fatigue*. Adapted by Laleh Bakhtiar from translations by O. Cameron and Mazar H. Shah. Great Books of the Islamic World. Chicago, IL: KAZI Publications.

————(2012) *Qanun fil-Tibb* (*The Canon of Medicine*) (*TCM*), vol. 1, *On Healthy Living: Managing the Elderly, Temperament Extremes and Environmental Changes*. Adapted by Laleh Bakhtiar from translations by O. Cameron and Mazar H. Shah. Great Books of the Islamic World. Chicago, IL: KAZI Publications.

————(2012) *Qanun fil-Tibb* (*The Canon of Medicine*) (*TCM*), vol. 1, *On Medicine and Its Topics*. Adapted by Laleh Bakhtiar from translations by O. Cameron and Mazar H. Shah. Great Books of the Islamic World. Chicago, IL: KAZI Publications.

————(2012) *Qanun fil-Tibb* (*The Canon of Medicine*) (*TCM*), vol. 1, *On the Breath*. Adapted by Laleh Bakhtiar from translations by O. Cameron and Mazar H. Shah. Great Books of the Islamic World. Chicago, IL: KAZI Publications.

————(2012) *Qanun fil-Tibb* (*The Canon of Medicine*) (*TCM*), vol. 1, *On the Causes of Illness* (*Etiology*). Adapted by Laleh Bakhtiar from translations by O. Cameron and Mazar H. Shah. Great Books of the Islamic World. Chicago, IL: KAZI Publications.

————(2012) *Qanun fil-Tibb* (*The Canon of Medicine*) (*TCM*), vol. 1, *On the Four*

Elements. Adapted by Laleh Bakhtiar from translations by O. Cameron and Mazar H. Shah.

——(2012) *Qanun fil-Tibb* (*The Canon of Medicine*) (*TCM*), vol. 1, *On the Four Humours*. Adapted by Laleh Bakhtiar from translations by O. Cameron and Mazar H. Shah. Great Books of the Islamic World. Chicago, IL: KAZI Publications.

——(2012) *Qanun fil-Tibb* (*The Canon of Medicine*) (*TCM*), vol. 1, *On the Temperaments*. Adapted by Laleh Bakhtiar from translations by O. Cameron and Mazar H. Shah. Great Books of the Islamic World. Chicago, IL: KAZI Publications.

——(2012) *Qanun fil-Tibb* (*The Canon of Medicine*) (*TCM*), vol. 1, *On the Pulse*. Adapted by Laleh Bakhtiar from translations by O. Cameron and Mazar H. Shah. Great Books of the Islamic World. Chicago, IL: KAZI Publications.

——(2012) *Qanun fil-Tibb* (*The Canon of Medicine*) (*TCM*), vol. 1, *On the Three Faculties*. Adapted by Laleh Bakhtiar from translations by O. Cameron and Mazar H. Shah. Great Books of the Islamic World. Chicago, IL: KAZI Publications.

——(2012) *Qanun fil-Tibb* (*The Canon of Medicine*) (*TCM*), vol. 1, *On Therapeutics: Diseases, Disorders, Obstructions, Swellings and Managing Pain*. Adapted by Laleh Bakhtiar from translations by O. Cameron and Mazar H. Shah. Great Books of the Islamic World. Chicago, IL: KAZI Publications.

——(2012) Poem on Medicine (*Urjuza fil tibb*): *A Textbook on Traditional Medicine*. Adapted by Laleh Bakhtiar. Great Books of the Islamic World. Chicago, IL: KAZI Publications.

——(2012). *Qanun fil-Tibb* (*The Canon of Medicine*: *Natural Pharmaceuticals*, vol. 2, *On Aphrodisiacs and their Medicinal Uses*. Compiled by Laleh Bakhtiar. Great Books of the Islamic World. Chicago, IL: KAZI Publications.

——(2012). *Qanun fil-Tibb* (*The Canon of Medicine*: *Natural Pharmaceuticals*, vol. 2, *On the Healing Properties of Minerals, Plants, Herbs and Animals*. Compiled by Laleh Bakhtiar. Great Books of the Islamic World. Chicago, IL: KAZI Publications.

——(2012). *Qanun fil-Tibb* (*The Canon of Medicine*: *Natural Pharmaceuticals*, vol. 2, *On Treating Arthritis and the Joints*. Compiled by Laleh Bakhtiar. Great Books of the Islamic World. Chicago, IL: KAZI Publications.

——(2012). *Qanun fil-Tibb* (*The Canon of Medicine*: *Natural Pharmaceuticals*, vol. 2, *On Treating Swellings and Pimples*. Compiled by Laleh Bakhtiar. Great Books of the Islamic World. Chicago, IL: KAZI Publications.

——(2012). *Qanun fil-Tibb* (*The Canon of Medicine*: *Natural Pharmaceuticals*, vol. 2, *On Treating the Alimentary Organs and Diet*. Compiled by Laleh Bakhtiar. Great Books of the Islamic World. Chicago, IL: KAZI Publications.

——(2012). *Qanun fil-Tibb* (*Canon of Medicine*: *Natural Pharmaceuticals*, vol. 2, *On Treating the Excretory Organs*. Compiled by Laleh Bakhtiar. Great Books of the Islamic World. Chicago, IL: KAZI Publications.

——(2012). *Qanun fil-Tibb* (*The Canon of Medicine*: *Natural Pharmaceuticals*, vol. 2, *On Treating the Organs of the Head*. Compiled by Laleh Bakhtiar.

Great Books of the Islamic World. Chicago, IL: KAZI Publications.

———(2012). *Qanun fil-Tibb* (*The Canon of Medicine*: *Natural Pharmaceuticals*, vol. 2, *On Treating the Respiratory Organs and the Chest*. Compiled by Laleh Bakhtiar. Great Books of the Islamic World. Chicago, IL: KAZI Publications.

———(2012). *Qanun fil-Tibb* (*The Canon of Medicine*: *Natural Pharmaceuticals*, vol. 2, *On Treating the Visual Organs*. Compiled by Laleh Bakhtiar. Great Books of the Islamic World. Chicago, IL: KAZI Publications.

———(2012). *Qanun fil-Tibb* (*The Canon of Medicine*: *Natural Pharmaceuticals*, vol. 2, *On Treating Wounds and Ulcers*. Compiled by Laleh Bakhtiar. Great Books of the Islamic World. Chicago, IL: KAZI Publications.

———(2013). *On Cardiac Drugs*. Adapted by Laleh Bakhtiar. Great Books of the Islamic World. Chicago: KAZI Publications.

———(2013). *On the Science of the Soul*. Adapted by Laleh Bakhtiar. Great Books of the Islamic World. Chicago: KAZI Publications.

Rumi, Jalal al-Din. (1898). *Divan-e Shams-e Tabrizi* 3:218. Translated by R. A. Nicholson. Cambridge, UK: Cambridge University Press.

Rumi, Jalal al-Din. (1906). *Masnavi*, 3:218. Translated by E. G. Browne, *A Literary History of Persia*. 4 vols. London, UK: T. F. Unwin.

Shabistari, Mahmud. (1923). *Gulshan-i Raz* lines 250-255. Translated by E. H. Whinfield.

SECONDARY SOURCES

al-Attas, Syed Muhammad Naquib. (1990). *The Nature of Man and the Psychology of the Human Soul* (NHS), Kusala Lumpur, Malaysia: ISTAC.

Bakhtiar, Laleh. (1993). *Moral Healer's Handbook*. Chicago IL: Institute of Traditional Psychoethics and Guidance.

———(1993). *Moral Healing Through the Most Beautiful Names*. Chicago: Institute of Traditional Psychoethics and Guidance.

———(2013). *Avicenna's Psychology*. Chicago IL: Institute of Traditional Psychoethics and Guidance.

———(2007). Translator of *The Sublime Quran*. Library of Islam. Chicago, IL: KAZI Publications.

Browne, E. G. (1906). *A Literary History of Persia*. 4 vols. London, UK: Luzac & Co.

Chittick, William. (2007). *Science of the Cosmos, Science of the Soul: The Pertinence of Islamic Cosmology in the Modern World* (WC). Oxford, UK: One World.

Corbin, Henri. (1960). *Avicenna and the Visionary Recitals*. Trasnlated by Willard R. Trask. Bollingen Series, v. 66. Princeton, NJ: Princeton University Press.

Davidson, Herbert. (1987) *Alfarabi, Avicenna, and Averroes, on Intellect*. New York and Oxford: Oxford University Press.

Druart, Therese-Anne. (1988) "The Soul and Body Problem: Avicenna and Descartes." In *Arabic Philosophy and the West*, ed. Therese-Anne Druart, 27-49. Washington, DC: Center for Contemporary Arab Studies, Georgetown

University.

Fakhry, Majid. (1991). *Ethical Theories in Islam* (MF). Leiden, Netherlands: E. J. Brill.

Goodman, Lenn E. (2006). *Avicenna* (LG). Ithaca, NY: Cornell University Press.

Hall, Robert E. (2004) "Intellect, Soul and Body in Ibn Sina: Systematic Synthesis and Development of the Aristotelian, Neoplatonic and Galenic Theories." In McGinnis, *Interpreting Avicenna*, 62-86

Hankinson, R. J. (2009). "Medicine and the Science of the Soul." *Can Bull Med Hist* 26(1):129-154.

Haque, Amber. (2004). "Psychology from an Islamic Perspective: Contributions of Early Muslim Scholars and Challenges to Contemporary Psychologists." *Journal of Religion and Health* (AH), 43(4):357-377.

Kamali, Mohammad Hashim. (2006). "Reading the Signs: A Quranic Perspective", *Islam & Science*, Winter, Volume 4, Number 2.

Lutz, Peter L. (2002). *The Rise of Experimental Biology: An Illustrated History.* New York, NY: Human Press.

Maher, Michael. (1982). *Psychology.* Bedford, MA: Magi Books.

McGinnis, Jon, ed. (2004) *Interpreting Avicenna: Science and Philosophy in Medieval Islam.* Leiden: E. J. Brill.

⸺(2010). *Avicenna.* (JM) Oxford, UK: Oxford University Press.

Nasr, Seyyed Hossein. (1976). *Islamic Science: An Illustrated Study* (*ISIS*). London, UK: World of Islam Festival.

⸺(1976). *Three Muslim Sages.* New York, NY: Caravan Books.

⸺and Oliver Leaman, eds. (1996). *History of Islamic Philosophy.* London and New York: Routledge.

⸺(1993). *An Introduction to Islamic Cosmological Doctrines* (*ICD*). Albany, NY: State University of New York Press.

⸺(2001). *Science and Civilization in Islam* (*SCI*). Chicago, IL: ABC International Group.

Okasha, A. C. R. (2001). "Mental Health and Psychiatry in the Middle East." *Eastern Mediterranean Health Journal* 7:336-347.

Sherif, Mohamed Ahmed. (1975). *Ghazali's Theory of Virtue.* Albany NY: State University of New York Press.

Yarsharter, Ehsan, ed. (1996-). *Encyclopedia Iranica*: Online Edition. New York, NY: Columbia Center for Iranian Studies.